MW01075220

CPR for The Grieving Heart

How I learned to love my life again

By Margaret Mary Stoiber

Moonbow Publications & Productions, LLC
Menomonee Falls, WI

Front Matter

Published in in the United States of America by Moonbow Publications
Printed in the United States of America by Ingram Spark
Catalog-in-Publication data for this book is available from the Library of Congress.
ISBN 978-1-7342798-8-7

Cover design by Sherry Levitsch
Artwork by Samuel Stoiber
Layout by Sue Carlson

Image Credits
Shaft of Wheat
Pearson Scott Foresman, Public Domain
https://commons.wikimedia.org/wiki/File:Barley_(PSF).png
The Intersexes – Separator – Note 2
Edward Irenaeus Prime-Stevenson, Public Domain
https://commons.wikimedia.org/wiki/File:The_Intersexes_-_Separator_-_Note_2.png

While the author has made every effort to provide correct internet addresses at the time of publication, neither the publisher nor the author assumes any responsibility for errors, or for changes that occur after publication. Further, the publisher does not have any control over and does not assume any responsibility for the author or third-party websites or their contents.

Are you or is someone you know struggling with the loss of a loved one this holiday season?

"CPR for the Grieving Heart" offers simple tools to guide one through the grieving process. It includes steps to opening your heart to love again, and natural ways to heal such as meditation, affirmations, essential oils and baths.

Margaret Stoiber is available for workshops, women's circles, chakradance and to lead guided meditation.

CPRforthegrievingheart.com

You don't have to feel so alone

Dedication

For Mark - I'll love you forever, too.

For our three children
Maddie, Sam, and Kate
My heart overflows with love for you, always

Author's Note

To my dear family and friends, thank you!

You have supported me and held me in your heart with much love throughout the years. It has been a long road and you have all helped me. Every act of kindness has brought me to where I am today and this has all played a role in my growth and recovery. I know if you had not been in my life, something would have been missing.

This is the latest version of my truth. I've written and rewritten this book many times. My story will continue to evolve as I learn and grow more, however I decided to stop here. I am quite shy and more than a little nervous about sharing my innermost thoughts with the world. However, with all of you supporting me, I know I am going to be all right.

I love you!!

Forward
by Madeline Stoiber

Look mom- I'm in a book! And it's yours!

Bad, but opportune, jokes aside, it's pretty rare you get an opportunity to write a forward in your mom's published book. That makes sense though, because my life has been a beautiful series of rarities all thanks to my mom

It's rare to grow up in a house where creativity, magic, and individuality are fostered from day one. It's rare your parents believe in and push you to pursue your dreams, no questions asked. It's rare you're taught the qualities of empathy, understanding, and patience are just as important as strength and perseverance. It's rare your family is able to stay together and grow stronger after a tragic loss. And it's really rare your mom turns the one of the hardest and most difficult moments in her life into a book to help others.

My mom does not see the world like everyone else. For her, even the darkest corners hold a chance to learn, grow, and become a more understanding person. This book will not only give you a peek into her unique perspective, but also a chance to read some of the words I heard growing up. Words that gave our family the foundation to heal, words that made me look within myself to grow, and words that guided me to become the successful woman I am today.

As you can see, my mom is a true rarity. I would be nowhere without the lessons I learned from her and the immense sacrifices she made. I hope this book finds a way to heal your heart, just like my mom healed mine.

Forward
by Kate Stoiber

As I am sure you will learn through reading this book, the author lost her husband unexpectedly one July day in 2010, leaving her with three children to raise on her own. I happen to be one of those children, the youngest one.

My brain was only ten years old when it was struck by grief and, to put it succinctly, I did not come out unscathed. The unexpected nature of my dad's passing short-circuited something in my brain into thinking that the next catastrophic event was always moments away. I developed severe anxiety that my mom was permanently in a state of danger. During any moment of separation, I would almost always become panicked that she had unexpectedly been taken from me just like my Dad. This was the darkest and loneliest time of my life.

Even the most understanding and patient people grew frustrated with my constant state of anxiety. There was one standalone though, one person who never judged me. One person who never called me crazy. One person who had to come home early from parties and answer fifty calls in the grocery store. One person who had to pick me up every day from school, so I didn't come to an empty house and panic. One person who refused to let me go through this alone. This person was my mom.

She felt the effects of my declining mental health the worst and she never once lost her patience. I would get anxious even when we were in the same house together, that somehow, she would be taken from me. Even then, she never, even for a moment, made me feel guilty for being shipwrecked by my grief.

If there is one person qualified to write advice for the ever-porous wound that grief inflicts, it is my mom.

Preface

Have you felt lost or forgotten since the passing of your loved one?

Are you searching for something, anything to help you feel better, yet you don't know what you are looking for?

Let me help.

I've created this guided interactive book for you.

I invite you to allow the flow of natural and divine healing into your heart.

Prologue

Here is my story.

In 2010, my life was everything I had ever dreamed of: I was still so in love with my handsome husband Mark after 22 years together. We had three healthy children, a beautiful home, and financial security.

Everything changed one sunny July morning.

The day began innocently: Mark, being the ultra-hard-working business owner he was, woke early and immediately jumped onto his laptop to send emails to others in his company. I arose a bit later and joined him in some coffee. We discussed the possibility of attending a music festival later that day.

A few minutes later, he stated he didn't feel well and went to lie down on the couch.

Then the inexplicable happened.

Without any warning or illness, Mark died suddenly in my arms of a pulmonary embolism, a blood clot in his lungs.

I literally woke up that day as one person and went to bed as someone else entirely.

For the next several months, people spoke to me and I often couldn't grasp what they were saying. I was watching my life and acting as a widow and mother of three, yet this new role was one I never imagined playing.

My life had become a nightmare.

As time went on, I did everything I could to heal. I read a multitude of books, I went to one-on-one grief therapy sessions, and joined an online community for widows and widowers. I flew to California, a world away, and attended a 3-day intensive group healing seminar. I even trained to become a grief counselor.

I learned so much.

I learned the world is full of wonderful people with unique stories and situations. Many have endured the traumatic passing of their loved ones and others have experienced the anguish of divorce, painful job losses, and debilitating illnesses and injuries.

In our society, we tend to know more about the physical heart than our emotional heart. Perhaps you have attended CPR classes? I expect that many of you could identify one or two symptoms of a heart attack. Defibrillators are now required in public buildings. However, there isn't a lot of awareness or education on how to speak with someone who is going through profoundly difficult and traumatic experiences. We don't always know what to say or how to offer just the right life-affirming words of encouragement. We have forgotten our true essence is love and don't know how to speak from the heart.

Because of all I've endured and experienced, I'd like to share with you some of what I've learned.

How? With a collection of simple exercises you can do at your own pace. These exercises are called "CPR for The Grieving Heart."

CPR stands for being Compassionate, being Present, and being Receptive. You do not need to visit a health care provider to receive this type of CPR, but you will need to do some simple reflections and basic activities on your own.

This workbook has three parts; the first is a series of grounding exercises to help you reconnect with yourself; the second part introduces and expands upon CPR; and the third is a series of exercises designed to help you incorporate CPR into your life as an ongoing practice.

Remember to move through this book at your own pace. The work you do in these exercises is for YOU - not for anyone else - and it is important for you to take the time you need to complete and process the exercises. The ideas and exercises may seem simple; and they can be transformative.

Some parts may resonate with you while others do not. Take what works for you and leave the rest.

You can do the exercises right in the book, on your computer, or in a notebook or journal. Choose what works best for you. You may even wish to have some colored pens at hand if you choose to work on paper. You may also wish to record some of the exercises so you can close your eyes and focus on the spoken words when you engage with them.

Part 1
Reconnecting with Yourself

Your Precious Heart

Do you remember?

When we are young, living authentically from our heart is so uncomplicated. We express our emotions easily and are always in the present moment.

Having fun is our only priority! We are filled with exuberance, spontaneity, joy, and innocence.

When faced with potentially new sticky situations, we immediately create a game and every part now becomes exciting.

Dancing, galloping, or skipping are how we move about. We cry profusely when we are sad and laugh unabashedly when we are happy. We always know how we feel.

We gravitate to what we love and run from what makes us frightened or uncomfortable.

We love our bodies and are constantly amazed with ourselves, no matter our size or shape.

We know what is right for US and are not afraid to let others know.

As we get older, we let societal standards and responsibilities into our hearts and minds and we become who we think we should be.

We forget who we are.

Ready to find out who you are?

Let's jump right in by identifying the important people in our lives.

Exercise: The Important People in My Life

Write in this book or get out whatever tool you're using to do the exercises.

Make a list of all of your loved ones: family members, friends, pets, in-laws, neighbors, and coworkers - everyone you love.

You can use the space on the next page if you wish. If you run out of room, write in the margins, on another sheet of paper, or whatever works for you!

Don't rush. Take a slow easy breath in, let it out, and take all the time you need.

You will come back to this list as you work through the exercises in this book.

If you need to take a break, go right ahead.

If you're ready, move on to the next chapter.

My Loved Ones

Did You Forget Anyone?

We ended the last section by taking an inventory of all the people you love. Let's continue looking. Who did you not include in your list?

Exercise – More Loved Ones

Slowly examine your list of loved ones.

Who did you forget? Add those people to your list.

Continue to add people as they come to mind.

Look again. Keep adding to your list.

Reflection

Take a moment to reflect on these questions.

- Do you see yourself anywhere on that list?
- Are YOU someone you love?
- Have you ever, at any point in your life, put yourself first?
- Why do you think this is?
- What is different now?
- Why is it different?
- Are you going to add yourself to your list of loved ones?
- Why or why not?

Really think about this - it's important because YOU are important.

Reflections on My Loved Ones

Most of us give, give, and give even more until we're empty. Does this sound familiar?

I went through this after my husband died. I gave and I gave and I gave until I realized something had to change or I was going to lose myself.

We cannot pour water from a cup that's empty.

To repeat: WE CANNOT POUR WATER FROM A CUP THAT IS EMPTY!

If we want to give to others, we have to fill ourselves up. Our cups need to be spilling and running over with so much tenderness that love is literally pouring out of us. When this happens we can easily and graciously give to others. But how, you ask yourself, how do I do this?

The answer is simple. We need to love ourselves.

Exercise: Deep breathing and visualization

If you haven't already done so, set your list of loved ones aside.
- Sit so you are comfortable and relaxed.
- Take 2-3 deep breaths, pulling the air in through your nose, allowing your belly to expand, and letting it out slowly through your nose or mouth.
- Read through the rest of this exercise, then close your eyes and picture a pet or a person you love. This may be your child or grandchild, a special niece or nephew, or neighbor. Picture this person at 5 or 6 years of age, until you have a crystal-clear image in your mind. Note if you are not close with a child, picture a pet or other person you love.
- Next, imagine the person you love lost their puppy. Think of how sad they would feel.
  - What would you say to that special person?
  - What would you do?

- o What would you offer?
- I invite you to visualize this and allow your emotions to flow.
- Now, open your eyes, and write down what you just imagined:
  - o the special kind words you wanted to say to the person or the things you would do to help them feel better.
  - o would you hug them?
  - o would you hold their hand?
- Write down all those extra sweet things you would do.

Let's call this list "How I Comfort with Love"

How I Comfort with Love

```



















```

Have you finished? Good! Set this list aside.

Take a break and come back with a clear mind when you are ready.

Let's switch gears and talk about how you talk to yourself.

Exercise: My Bad Day Experience

Think about the last time you were frustrated or had a bad day.
- What happened?
- How did you feel?
- What words did you say to yourself?
- Did you say anything to anyone else?
- Do you regret anything you said?

Write a few sentences about the experience.

My Bad Day Experience

When going through difficult times, I used to talk to myself and say things like:

- "Stop crying. You don't have time to cry."
- "Suck it up, buttercup."
- "You can cry later. You don't have time right now. You need to be strong."

I say these mean words to myself during difficult times.

Exercise: Mean Things I Say to Myself

Make another list called "Mean Things I Say to Myself." Write down all the angry, mean thoughts and voices in your head.

Mean Things I Say to Myself

Once you've finished this list, take out the list "How I Comfort with Love."

Look at the heartfelt words you would say or the things you would do for that special child or animal.

Reflection

Compare what you wrote in "How I Comfort with Love" with what you wrote in "Mean Things I Say to Myself."

- Have you ever said those sweet things to yourself when you're sad?
- Have you ever given yourself that comfort?
- Did you give yourself any special time?
- Or do you tell yourself to yourself to suck it up, buttercup or get going - you don't have time to cry?
- How do you speak to yourself?
- Why don't you deserve the same loving kindness you would give a young child?

Reflect on the difference in how you speak to yourself when you're hurting versus how you speak to others who are hurting.

Differences in My Speaking

Each of us is still a child inside. Each of us deserves care and comfort. If we can give it so freely to others, why can't we give it to ourselves?

Exercise: All the People I Love

- List all the people you love inside the heart on the next page, and this time include yourself.

- Once you've listed all your loved ones, including yourself, in the heart, add in the kind loving words, beautiful phrases, and sweet gestures you would use to comfort a child or animal. You may wish to use a happy color for this part of the exercise.

- Now write in the mean words you said to yourself. You may choose to use an unhappy color for these.

- Place your hands on your heart, breathe deeply in and out, and send love to that part of you that is unhealed and wounded inside. Do this for several minutes until you truly feel your love for yourself.

- Love every part of YOU so much that eventually you do not say any mean things to yourself.

Have fun with this exercise. Be kind to yourself – notice and let go of any judgment – allow the love to flow to and from you.

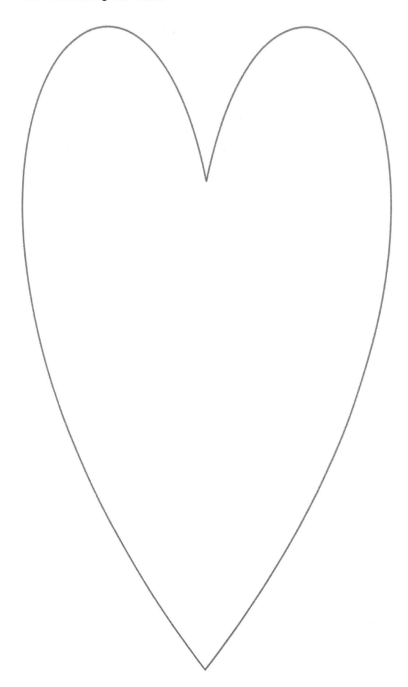

Reflection

How do you feel?

You've just created a simple new plan for self-care. Take a screen shot of the heart and use it as the background of your phone, place it near your mirror, or put it wherever you can see it every day.

Practice – Love yourself!

Every day, speak to yourself with these tender loving words and embrace the precious child inside of you.

Part 2
CPR

Being <u>C</u>ompassionate
Being <u>P</u>resent
Being <u>R</u>eceptive

23
Part 2: CPR Concepts

Being Compassionate

Are you ready to learn some CPR? How to be compassionate? How to be present? How to be receptive?

Let's start with compassion.

I used to think compassion was easier to give to others than to myself.

Maybe it was from my long history of being a nurse. Did nursing require me to have compassion? Was compassion just part of the job?

Or perhaps having a compassionate heart was part of my role in being a loving mom, wife, daughter, sister, and friend?

However, everything changed after Mark died.

When I say everything changed, I literally mean almost all aspects of my life were fundamentally different.

Here are some ways I changed:
● I now had to eat different foods just to avoid stomach pains,
● I required much more rest time just to feel normal,
● many of my interests changed,
● my ability to focus decreased,
● my need for time alone increased, and
● so on and so on.

I had to restructure how I spent my time - and then learn how to not feel guilty for putting my needs first or disappointing anyone.

I began to rethink my relationship with our Heavenly Creator at about that same time.

As I pondered the possibility that our Heavenly Creator is filled with love and loves everyone unconditionally, I wondered where my feelings of guilt, judgement, and shame about being myself were coming from.

I questioned why I felt I had to be everything to everyone and why I dismissed my own needs. Why was I not loving myself unconditionally?

The more I thought about it, the more I thought about my own children.

As a parent, I want my children to experience life as complete joy and delight!!

I am so very confident that is how our Heavenly Creator wants us to be so we lead joyful lives!!!

Exercise: What Brings You Joy?

What brings you joy?

Sometimes people have a hard time answering this because they are so conditioned to take care of their families and fulfill their career responsibilities before caring for themselves.

Perhaps there is another way to look at it:
- What do you love doing?
- What makes you happy?
- What makes you feel like a child again?
- If money was no object and you could do absolutely anything, what would you choose?

Create a list of what brings you Joy

Things that bring me joy

Take a look at your list.
- Did you have difficulty listing anything?
- How often do you spend your day doing any of these activities?
- Do you impose conditions on giving yourself time to experience joy and unconditional love?

Reflect on how you experience joy

Another way to be compassionate with ourselves is to allow ourselves to express all our emotions freely, however that looks.

These pains you feel are messengers.
Listen to them.
Rumi

Have you ever been speaking with someone when something they said set you off and the next thing you knew, you were shouting at each other? Why did this happen? Because of the buried emotions inside of you.

For some reason in our society, tears and crying are seen as weakness. It seems like yelling, cursing, or being inebriated are acceptable ways to express emotions while crying is looked down upon.

Tears are one of the most primal ways we soothe ourselves. Crying helps to release oxytocin and endorphins. These chemicals help you feel better and promote a sense of well-being.

Reflection

Do you allow yourself to cry? Why or why not?

Expressing Emotion

Learning to express our emotions is another way we can be compassionate with ourselves. We can express our emotions in a number of ways. Find a way that works well for you.

Write things down

I used to love to read. After my husband died, I began to read again and I started taking notes. I didn't know what I was taking notes on, but thoughts would come to me. I was compelled to write these thoughts down: on napkins and on my phone. I'd even send emails to myself!. Why? Because I was trying to cope with heavy, difficult emotions and I needed some way to express them. If I hung on to them, they were going to make me crazy.

Keep a personal journal

Another way to express and process our emotions is to keep a personal journal. Writing in a journal allows you to express your feelings privately and get them out of your head. Later, you can go back to discover how far you've traveled in your healing journey.

Create or listen to music

Creating music is another great method to express our feelings. Singing is an amazing way to allow our feelings to flow. It doesn't matter how good or bad you think you sound - that's what long car rides and showers are for. There's nothing like cranking some tunes and belting out a song in full voice.

When I was a child, I used to run around the house saying, "EEEEEE." I remember doing this and thinking it was fun. You know what? The "ee" tone as heard in the word "be" is actually part of a practice known as vocal toning, or Nada Yoga, and helps stimulate the brain. Look into this further if sound therapy appeals to you.

Have you ever written a song? Maybe you created something as a child? Gather your ideas and put together a story of how you want to feel in your life. Make up a tune that fits the story. Whenever you can, sing your own little song for well-being and happiness.

If possible, include "I am" statements. One example: "I am joyful and my heart shines bright, I am filled with God's loving light." Sing it to yourself out loud and proud.

Create Art

Creating art, for example by painting freely, is another way to express yourself.

What would it feel like to create art or sing for the joy and not for the perfection?

Allow yourself to get lost in the colors, shapes, and textures. Allow yourself to be IN the art. Remember how fun art class was in grade school? Think of being creative as play time. You might be surprised how fun it can be!

Move your body

Another way to express your emotions is through movements such as walking, running, biking, chi gong and dancing. I try to dance every day. It doesn't matter if I dance on a dance floor or in my car or on a sidewalk. It just feels good and I don't who cares who sees me! Have you ever danced like no one is watching? If not - try it out. It's liberating.

Talk to yourself

We all love to talk. A wise person once told me, "Margaret, a good way to get your emotions out is to put some earbuds in, connect them to your phone, and talk to yourself as you walk along. Just talk to yourself. People will think you're in a conversation with someone else and you can just talk away." They don't need to know you're in a conversation with yourself.

Talking to yourself is healthy. I do it all the time. Talking is a good way to express yourself.

Let's Review

Giving compassionate care to our hearts is simple.

Respect that child who lives inside you. Gently ask yourself, what do you need today?

Remember to love yourself unconditionally. This involves giving yourself time for joyful activities and permission to limit other activities.

Allow yourself to express your emotions in a way that relieves and comforts you whether you cry, journal, sing, paint, move, or talk to yourself.

Being Present

We all hear a lot about being 'present' in today's world. Almost every talk show guru talks about this concept. You can find lots of YouTube videos discussing how to "be present."

Basically, being present is being in the moment – not looking back to the past or forward into the future. It is being with whatever is happening right now, in this moment.

As I look back, I remember having a hard time with being present and mindful, at least initially, after Mark died.

I was often exhausted, with three grieving children to care for and numerous other worries. My emotional state wasn't great and I felt lonely and confused. Many times, I found myself either longing for the past or worrying about the future.

However, by not being present, I was missing bill payments, losing important papers, and getting off schedule. I was always a step behind. The impact of not being present made me miss my old life even more.

At some point, I stumbled upon a guided meditation track and discovered the power of being present through meditation. The track has binaural beats, which is basically a fancy way of saying it hypnotizes you as sounds enter each ear independently.

From my very first 30-minute session using binaural beats, I was able to fully relax! It was such a relief in my dark days. I began to find ways to meditate whenever I could. I eventually got to the point of looking forward to my daily meditation. I still meditate 11 years later.

Meditation is a wonderful tool to help you to experience your life in a more relaxed and loving state.
Please understand meditation is a practice. The goal is for you to feel in harmony with the universe rather than worry about achieving the perfect lotus position.

Meditation is beneficial in many ways. One of the most important is that meditation allows you to become aware of your breathing. Breathing is essential to meditative practice and also to the basic functioning of our bodies.

To clarify:
● Our bodies need a constant supply of oxygen to live, which we get through breathing.
● When we do not have enough oxygen, our brain gets a message to breathe rapidly, or hyperventilate, to pull more oxygen into the lungs.
● Hyperventilating, which is rapid breathing, may cause us to feel anxious.
● Being anxious can then cause us to breathe even more shallowly, potentially increasing the urge to hyperventilate.

You can see the vicious cycle.

Our Creator designed our bodies so that when we breathe deeply and slowly, we bring enough oxygen to our cells. When our bodies are well-oxygenated, a different message goes to our brain that allows the brain to move into an alpha rhythm. Alpha rhythms cause us to feel relaxed and loved by our Creator.

Thus, deep breathing feels wonderful!

Let's take a moment to practice deep breathing.

Practice: Deep Breathing

- Sit comfortably with your back straight and shoulders relaxed.
- Close your eyes and place your hands on your lower abdomen.
- Feel your abdomen rise and fall as the air moves in and out of your lungs.
- Breathe slowly in through your nose.
- Open your mouth and exhale.
- Sometimes it feels good to make an "ahhh" sound as you exhale with your mouth open.
- Some people prefer to breathe deeply in and out through their noses only.
- Continue to do this for a few minutes and relax into the moment.
- When you feel peaceful and relaxed, do the next exercise.

As you become comfortable with regular deep breathing and its effectiveness, I encourage you to explore alternative techniques, such as box breathing, and find what suits you best.

Exercise: Moments in Life

- In the left column, reflect on your recurring memories of life before you lost your beloved.
- Make a list of your absolute favorite memories, as well as those moments in time that cause your heart to ache.
- Take all the time you need.
- Use the middle column to create a list of the concerns and worries you have for the future.
- What causes you to lay awake at night?
- Use the right column to describe how you want your future to look.
- What do you want to do?
- Who do you want in your life?
- What will give you joy and happiness?

- How do you want to be in the world?
- Think of some actions you could do to help bring this to life.

Recurring Memories	Concerns and Worries	How I Want My Future to Look

Again, there's no rush to complete this exercise. Be patient with yourself. This exercise may take hours or days to complete.

Exercise: Stick Figure

After you've finished your lists of recurring memories, worries for the future and ideas for your new life, draw a stick figure of yourself, with a face and arms open wide. If you're using the image below, add a face, hair, and any other of your traits you want to include.

On your left arm, draw a purse or perhaps a backpack. In your right hand, draw a picture frame. Over the midsection of your body, draw a present.

What does the stick figure represent?
- The bag on your left arm represents the past.
- The picture frame represents the future.
- The gift represents the present.

After Mark died, I spent too much time in the past. I couldn't stop thinking about how everything was so much better when he was alive or wondering whether if I had done something differently, Mark would still be with me. If you spend too much time in the past, you become sad because it's gone and you also may regret things you said or did.

I now like to think my memories of Mark are like special coins in my purse —valuable and always with me. Whenever I want or need to, I can take them out and remember those times. I can learn from the past. I can always share those memories with my children and I can put them aside as I learn to live in the present.

Now let's look at your list of worries about the future.

Perhaps when you spend too much time in the future, you may say things like, "When this happens, I'll be happy" or "What will I do if this happens?" Statements like this can make you anxious and stop you from living in the present. Life occurs in the present moment, not the future or the past.

We cannot create our future by living in the past or by anxiously worrying about the future.

Consider a new way to view the future.

You can create your future by taking small steps daily and visualizing what you would like to see as if it is in a picture frame. Then let your ideas go like the floating seeds from a dandelion and allow the divine to bring about your wishes for a new life.

Where you want to be is in the present. Remember the divine can only speak to you in this now moment. The present is the present. Get it?

How do we stay present? One way is to refer to the stick figure you just drew as a reminder to be conscious of whether you are living in the past, present, or future.

Whenever you find yourself spending too much time in the past, feeling sad, or worrying about your future, you can use your own body as a guide to return to the present.

Exercises to stay in the present:

Instead of allowing anxious thoughts to loop incessantly in your head, use one of the exercises below to bring yourself back to the present moment.

Use this list of exercises as a resource when your thoughts overwhelm you. Try each one and then find what works best for you.

Start each exercise by closing your eyes and taking three deep breaths. The breath contains life-sustaining oxygen.

Exercise 1:
- Ask Jesus or your spiritual advisor to show you what is important for you to see in this moment.
- Open your eyes and take in your surroundings.
- Really look at what is around you.
- Notice colors, textures, shades, etc.
- You can only "see" in the present moment.

Exercise 2:
- Keep your eyes closed and focus on the scents around you.

- What do you notice?
- You can only "smell" in the present moment.

Exercise 3:
- Open your eyes and look into the mirror.
- What are you really happy about today? Say or sing It!!
- What are you especially grateful for? Speak to your reflection in loving gratitude
- Say whatever words YOU need to hear today.
- Speak out loud to your loved ones to let them know how much they mean to you.
- Thus, "speaking" can only be done in the present moment.

Exercise 4:
- Feel your heartbeat.
- Do you know how to find your pulse?
- The easiest way is to place your index and middle finger (don't use your thumb because your thumb has its own pulse) between the bone and tendon on the thumb side of your wrist to feel your radial artery.
- Another way is to place your hand on your heart and feel your heart beating. In a sense, this is the Creator sustaining you.
- Feel this life saving movement of blood in your body.
- Thus, "touch" can only be done in the present moment.

Exercise 5:
- With your eyes closed, listen to what is going on around you.
- Now try to hear any sounds from the next room.

- Pause.
- Do any advice or insights pop into your head?
- Thus, "listening" and "intuition" are only found in the present moment.

Exercise 6:
- Going outside can be a delightful way to keep yourself mindful.
- The varying temperatures, colors, wind speeds, and sounds of nature will combine to give you a multi-sensory dose of the present moment.
- The sweet song of birds in the morning can be especially therapeutic.
- Hear and feel the beauty around you.
- Thus, "hearing" and "feeling" can only be done in the present moment.

Exercise 7:
- If the weather permits, take your shoes and socks off and place your bare feet on the earth.
- This is called grounding and it is a wonderful way to decompress and release stress.
- Try to spend at least 30 minutes like this.
- Thus, "grounding" can be a way to be in the present moment.

Exercise 8:
Humming is a rather unique way to give yourself a little tune up for reconnecting with the present moment.
- Keep your eyes closed.

- As you hum, gently cover each ear with your hands.
- Feel the humming vibrate within your head.
- You can practice with creating different tones, such as om, ham, yam, ram, vam and lam.*
- Try sending a healing intention with this tone to an area of your body that feels tight or is in pain.
- Thus, "humming" can be a way to be in the present moment.

*If you're interested, a simple search for the sounds of the 7 chakras or energy centers in the body will help you understand more about these tones.

Exercise 9:
- Can you sense your body needs to move in a certain way?
- I seem to find myself making slow hip circles or rocking back and forth often.
- Thus, "movement" can be another way to be in the present.

In summary, being in the present moment is as simple as breathing.

The key is within you. If you forget, just look in the mirror, take a deep breath, and go!

Being Receptive

One day the finality of losing Mark hit me, as they say, "like a ton of bricks."

I remember exactly where I was. It was about five months after his passing. I was in a Kohl's store and the song "I'll be Home for Christmas" came over the store's PA system.

Many beloved scenes and feelings entered my mind: Christmas celebrations from the past, our own secret Christmas Eve gift exchange tradition, and the fun we had conspiring to create unique surprises for our children. It all hit me in the gut in that moment.

I realized I would never ever hear his voice, see his smile, or laugh again with him. How could Christmas go on without him?

I became so distraught I couldn't move. My eyes flooded with tears and I wanted to disappear to stop that pain. It felt like it would never end.

Somehow I managed to stumble out of the store and cried in my car for hours. Waves of loneliness washed over me.

This song triggered many deeply buried emotions.

Exercise: Reminders

Have you ever experienced a similar reaction - when the finality of your loved one 's passing is all too real? It sometimes helps to write your feelings down.

Reflect on that experience.

Although the experience I had in Kohl's was heart-wrenching, it started a slow change inside me. No longer did I wear the cloak of Mark's protection and love around me. I now had to face the world alone and on my terms.

The first thing I noticed was a sense the world around me was more responsive than I realized.

When faced with challenges with my children, I began to almost hear Mark's thoughts in my head. I could feel what he wanted me to do in most situations.

I began to spend more and more time in solitude and in my thoughts, eventually thinking about the meaning of life, the mysteries of death, and the purpose of it all.

It slowly dawned on me I was receiving signs from the divine and possibly even from Mark.

However, my many years of religious and nursing education told me this couldn't be true. Yet in my heart it felt right.

I began to question everything:

- Did God only speak to prophets during biblical times?
- Does God only speak to priest and rabbis?
- Could God be speaking to me through nature?
- Did God place signs like the Fibonacci sequence in nature for us to see and receive?
- Could the God who created our vast diverse universe and tiny perfect intricate snowflakes find a way to communicate with me?

My heart joyfully sang, "Yes!!"

I also pondered the possibility of an unseen spiritual team around me, consisting of God, Jesus, Angels, departed grandparents, and Mark, loving and guiding me daily.

Was part of my unhappiness due to the fact I was looking for Mark here on earth, in the places he used to be, when he was now a spirit?

Was I essentially looking for Mark in all the wrong places? Did I need to open my heart and reevaluate my views of the spirit world?

Receiving Messages from the Divine

Since my husband's passing, I have received several messages from him, some in dreams.

There was a period when I was ill for many months; I could not get well. I had just completed a 12-week refresher course in hospice care nursing. Perhaps my illness was prolonged because I had been surrounded by death, but whatever the cause, I became extremely ill. I suffered one virus after another without relief.

Three, almost four months later, when I began to show signs of recovery, I made my family a special dinner. I was feeling like myself, went to bed, and my husband came to me in a dream. It was very brief. He was standing in the kitchen, wearing jeans and a button-down plaid shirt, and he said, "It's nice to see you dancing in the kitchen again." When I woke up, do you know what? I realized it had been months since I had danced in my kitchen!

I know that he really visited, that he was aware I'd been sick, and was giving me hope. It felt absolutely wonderful and in my heart I know it was a genuine message. I believe our loved ones can connect with us (it's heaven, after all!), so I believe in the afterlife. I received the blessing of this dream. Dreams are one way the divine connects with us.

We may also receive signs from the divine through music:

Here is one example:

My mother had been ill for several months; in the hospital, off to rehab, then back to the hospital. She had sepsis, a sometimes-fatal infection of the entire body, and she was very ill. Death seemed to be in the air and it was dragging me down. One day while I was grocery shopping, music was playing in the store and thoughts were going through my head of not being ready to lose someone again. Suddenly, I became aware of the song playing in the background. The words were, "Don't you worry, child, Heaven's got a plan for you. Don't you worry, child, Heaven's got a plan for you."

I immediately realized the song had been playing for several minutes and I had not been aware of it. It was as if someone turned up the volume, took my hand, pointed me in the right direction, and opened my ears. And I heard it, receiving the message from the divine. I felt loved and comforted and I knew this was a gift from above.

Another sign from the divine can be an unexpected phone call from a friend when you really need one. Perhaps your friend says to you, "You know, I was just thinking about you." How did that friend know you needed that call? And at just the right moment? Do you think Jesus or your Heavenly Creator whispered your name in your friend's ear? I do.

Many people believe in receiving signs from their loved ones through numerology. They report seeing special number sequences that are significant.

I ask YOU, when you feel good inside, when you feel warm-hearted, loved, and lifted spiritually, how can it not be signs from Heaven?

Exercise: Have you received messages?

- Have you ever received a message from your loved one?
- In what way did they connect with you?
- How did you feel?

Reflection on receiving messages

Believing and Receiving

I slowly began to realize I had to believe in order to receive and allow all the divine love that was graciously being shown to me.

Love is all around us and there are many ways to receive.

Initially, after Mark passed I found comfort in a park near my house. It was perfect; there was a half mile loop around a lagoon and plenty of ducks and geese and others enjoying the scenery. No one knew me or noticed the tears that gushed down my sunburned cheeks. Walking fast helped to curb some of my anxiety and I strangely found solace among strangers and nature and feeling like I was part of it all.

As time went on, I became more aware of our Mother Earth and all the ways she shares her love. At first, I noticed how many times I saw hearts in nature, in odd random ways; markings on a birch tree, a perfectly shaped leaf that just so happened to fall on my path while walking, a special stone on the road and once a pile of leaves shaped like a heart on my driveway, and on and on. Whenever I looked, I saw love and I appreciated it all.

I saw exquisite beauty everywhere. Sunsets, sunrises, vibrant colors in the rainbows, gorgeous smelling flowers, every part of nature felt as though it was created for my enjoyment.

I continued to receive the gifts of nature. There was a time when I needed something to help me relax and that's when I discovered lavender essential oil. Just a few drops of this beautiful scent and I become a marshmallow.

Did you know it takes three pounds of lavender flowers to create one tiny 15ml bottle of Lavender essential oil?

I started to learn about the amazing benefits of essential oils. They are powerful and very healing. One drop of an essential oil has approximately 40 million-trillion molecules and it crosses the blood brain barrier in our brain. Within minutes of applying this oil, I often feel relaxed.

Another way to receive nature is through enjoying herbal tea. There is something so sweet and relaxing when sipping tea. Herbal teas have many therapeutic benefits. Also, taking time to relax and go slower is pretty awesome, too.

I started the practice of being in nature as much as I could. I began to crave long walks where I didn't have to talk or explain myself. Watching the seasons change became my new favorite pastime. I became interested in observing wildlife more. Time in the forest soothed my soul and allowed my dense, heavy emotions to settle. I felt loved and nurtured.

In getting materials ready for this book, I came upon a description of a practice used by Aboriginal Indians called dadirri, which means deep listening of the land and still awareness in nature.

Now, whenever I am faced with troubling concerns or frustrations, I grab my shoes and my puppy Beau and we head for the forest to do some dadirri. I always come back refreshed and with a clear head.

Exercise: When is the last time you were in nature?

- When was the last time you interacted with nature?
- What did you do?
- How did you feel after?
- How do you receive nature?

Reflection on being in nature

Practice: Receive Sunflower Meditation

Our earthly family of the sun, moon, stars, trees, animals, and plants are always looking for ways to care for us and love us.

I invite you to read the meditation below. You may wish to record it so you can keep your eyes closed. I'm going to have a more detailed recording of this on my website: cprforthegrievingheart.com.

Go outside on a warm sunny day and experience the visualization my words create. Find a nice meadow or grassy spot where you will not be disturbed. If the weather does not allow you to be outside, find a comfortable place inside.

Meditation

- Lay down on your back
- Close your eyes
- Feel the warmth of the sun
- Breathe deeply in and out
- Surrender to your breath and allow your body to relax into the ground
- Allow Mother earth to hold you
- Place your hands on your heart
- Breathe slowly through this space
- Think about all the people you love
- Feel the love well up inside your heart
- Appreciate all the love and blessings in your life
- Continue to breathe slowly
- Visualize your heart as a closed sunflower bud deep inside your chest
- See a tiny yellow flicker of light inside the flower
- Keep breathing slowly in and out
- With each breath, the flower slowly opens and the light inside your heart glows brighter

- Feel the sun's warmth overhead as it sends golden rays of healing and light into your chest
- The sun and your heart share one light
- You are sharing your love light with the world
- Your heart and sunflower are now completely open
- Receive the outpouring of love and kindness
- Keep your heart open and share your heart light with the world
- Now take your arms and wrap them around you
- You are part of The One who has created it all
- You are loved

Once you've completed the meditation, take a few minutes to reflect on your experience.

- How do you feel?
- What was it like to engage in this meditation?

Reflection on the meditation

53
Part 2: CPR Concepts

Let's Review

Remember to be compassionate.

Remember that finding care for your wounded heart is easy. You have everything you need, without technology, special books, diplomas, degrees, or experts. It's all within you.

Remember to choose your self-talk carefully and be gentle with yourself. What words would you use or things would you do for your niece or nephew?

Remember the list you created. This list is the new way you care for yourself: wrap these positive prompts around you by putting them in your phone, or by putting written notes in your purse or on your pillow. Let them remind you.

Remember to keep your cup filled if you want to be able to help others. You CANNOT pour from an empty cup. If you are empty, you have nothing to give.

Remember to love yourself unconditionally and find ways to do joyful activities daily. Like a toddler, feel into what are the right activities for you. Remember to know yourself best and how to spend your time.

Remember to invite creative expression into your everyday life. Don't "save" those creative goals for "someday." Do something creative every day. Sing in your shower. Dance in your car. Create with color. Write. Blow soap bubbles. Every day, do whatever creative thing gives you a feeling of joy and allows you to release helpless, depressive feelings.

Remember to be present.

Remember the drawing of your body. Spending too much time is the past may have you become sad. Visit the past, with all of its memories, and use it as a place to learn.

Don't live in the past. Don't spend too much time in the future.

The future is for making plans, setting goals, anticipating. You shouldn't spend too much time there because you can't control the future. Spending too much time there will only make you anxious.

Remember to breathe in the Creator's love for you. Find your favorite of the exercises for the present and use them daily.

- Use your eyes to seek beauty in your surroundings
- Use your ears for truly listening
- Use your voice in gratitude
- Be in the moment

Remember the present IS a present.

Remember the grace of receiving

Remember to believe and receive messages from your beloved however they manifest. Listen for guidance when you need it. Your loved one wants to communicate with you.

Lastly, remember the joy of receiving from nature. There is an abundance of beauty and plant life to care for your body and soul. Open your heart as a sunflower in the sun, let it come to you, and give that love back to yourself and the world.

Are you ready?

CPR Exercises

The Bench

When we lose someone, we might begin thinking deeply about our ancestors who passed before us.

We might wonder about their suffering and their losses. How did they manage to survive? What did they do?

We might even wonder if they are aware of the current life challenges we are facing or if they are still praying for us.

My many solitary walks led me to this exercise. When was the last time you sat on a bench in a park? Have you ever?

Today, I'd like you to do that, weather permitting.

Exercise: Ask for help with your challenges

- Find a park bench in a quiet, comfortable place.
- If it's not possible to sit on a park bench, place an empty chair near you.
- Quiet your thoughts.
- Close your eyes.
- Breathe deeply.
- Invite your heavenly creator to be present in this moment.
- Keep breathing.
- Ask who you need to hear from.
- Continue to be conscious of your breathing.
- Wait... wait for a thought to float into your head.
- Whose face do you see?
- What memory comes in?
- Wait and stay with your breathing.
- What message comes through?

Reflection on your experience

The first time I did this exercise, my Grandma Mary popped in. My under-5-ft-tall Croatian Grandma who loved baking and taught me the phrase "make do."

Grandma was a busy mom of four during the Great Depression. If we discovered we didn't have enough sugar to make her famous walnut potica, we would make do and add some applesauce instead. It always worked out!

As I thought about her and pondered these memories, it dawned on me that I always end conversations with my family by saying, "I love you." I do this because after suddenly losing my beloved, it became quite clear that we never know when any of our conversations will be the last with anyone.

The feeling I got was Grandma was proud of me.

She was proud of me for offering this loving communication to my children and she thought it was really important. I also got the feeling Grandma Mary showed her love by "doing" while alive, and now understands some people need verbal affirmation.

She thanked me.

I thanked her.

I realized she still loved me and was concerned for me. It also dawned on me I probably have many relatives in Heaven who are rooting for me and my children.

This felt wonderful!

Exercise: Who's sitting on the bench with you?

Who wants to come sit on the bench with you? Maybe you have a message from a dear grandparent or relative.

- Did anyone visit? Who?
- What messages did you receive or send?
- How do you feel?
- Who else do you want to hear from?

Reflection on your experience

Flashback Remedy

Do you ever have flashbacks of your loved one? Does a particular image find its way into your head and, no matter what, just stick there like a giant piece of gum on your shoe?

I do. I used to frequently see the image of Mark laying on the metal hospital stretcher - cold, blue, and still. Over and over. I couldn't get this sight or that hospital smell out of my mind.

Over time, I learned to push these memories down and used the distractions of caring for kids, carpooling, illness, and music to keep them at bay. I would do anything I could to not feel and reflect back on that moment.

These flashbacks continued until one day, while in a deep meditation, I ventured back to that moment - that frozen in time space where my life became a living nightmare – and I saw my beloved still, cold and blue.

I somehow went back in time and became me again.

I stepped back into my body, and recalled my thoughts, all the numbness, and the feeling of floating above the scene.

I felt my stomach tighten.

I felt myself quietly panic.

I realized this was the beginning of my stomach issues.

It started with fear in this exact moment.

I then made myself stand behind me. I wrapped my arms around myself and told myself repeatedly that I was going to make it, that things would be all right, and that I could do it.

Somehow, this shifted something inside me. Constantly pushing this memory down was exhausting, and now that I no longer feared this nightmarish place in time, I felt lighter. My stomach issues have improved. I now see this recurring memory was showing me an area of my life that needed healing.

Reflection

What is your flashback memory?

Exercise: Give Yourself the Gift of You

- Find a quiet place.
- Close your eyes.
- Relax and breathe deeply.
- Ask Jesus, your Heavenly Creator and Angels to be with you in this moment.
- Hold your hands out and ask your Angels to place a photo album in your hands.
- Open the album and look at the image you've tried to forget.
- Ask your spiritual advisor what you need to remember from this particular moment.
- Wait for answers. If it feels right, go back to that moment and say to yourself what you needed in that moment.
- What do you now know that perhaps you might have needed back then?
- What did you need to hear at that time?

- Reflect back and give yourself the gift of "you" today. Send lots of love to that place and time.

Reflection

- How do you feel now when you remember this moment?
- Have your flashbacks decreased?

Final Gifts

The moment a loved ones passes imprints in your memory bank forever.

What you did immediately before, things your loved one might have said, the look of the room, special smells, and all the little details are forever etched into your consciousness.

My father died in 2007 and I can still recall the flowers sitting by his bed, a beautiful bouquet of red roses and purple wildflowers.

When Mark died in 2010, I didn't realize it at the time, but Mark actually died in my arms after I called 911 and before the ambulance arrived.

In that moment, he gave me a glimpse of a gift so precious, it's hard for me to talk about, even now.

Here is the scene:

Mark collapsed without warning one sunny July morning as he was getting ready to leave for work.

He then called my name.

I ran to his side.

Mark next said his last words to me, "Margaret Mary, I will love you forever."

With that, he closed his eyes.

I was confused. I checked for a pulse, I screamed, and I attempted resuscitation.
I called 911.

As I tried reviving him, Mark opened his eyes one last time.

He stared straight ahead, not seeing me, but seeing somewhere or someone beyond my shoulder.

Mark opened his eyes wide and after a moment they got even bigger and he slowly asked, "Who are you?"

He then closed his eyes for the last time and was non-responsive.

The ambulance came soon after that.

Mark's final gift to me was peace.

Peace means seeing a glimpse of eternity.

Peace means there is an afterlife.

Peace means absolute proof of a loving, caring, creator who came to meet my late husband in the last few breaths of his life.

Was it to reassure him? To comfort me?

Reflection

Spend a moment and reflect back on your loved one's death and last moments.

- What did you see?
- What do you know differently now?
- What new understandings do you have?
- New revelations?

- What was your loved ones lasting gift to you?
- How do you live your life differently?

Light a candle and reflect….

Can you hear me now?

I have always been fascinated with sound.

Relatives from my mom's side of the family told a story of when I was young so many times, I can almost see it myself:

Apparently, when I was 3 or 4 we were at a family party. Someone handed me a small transistor radio and I proceeded to dance around the gathering with the radio glued to my ear.

My love for music and movement continued with dance and Zumba.

After Mark passed, I found myself using music to help relieve my sadness. Songs like, "Moon River," "Remember When," and "My Sweet Lady" are a few that can easily bring me to tears.

Later I discovered the many ways music can heal.

One day, out of curiosity, I attended a gong bath. I wasn't sure what to expect. I had a sprained puffy ankle at the time and wondered what effects the gong would have on it.

The music was deeply healing!! Wow! The vibrations of the gongs went through my body and I felt as though I was in the next dimension of existence.

The next day my ankle was completely healed!

I now own several tuning forks and crystal singing bowls. The fun I have of tuning in, setting intentions, and playing to heal is one of my favorite ways to honor myself.

Do you like music? Have you noticed how certain songs can uplift and energize you? Which ones? How often do you listen to these tunes?

Can you name some songs that help you to release your emotions?

Do you own any instruments? If not, explore a music store to see if any instrument appeals to you.

Look for an opportunity to attend a gong bath or crystal bowl meditation.

Reflection

How do you feel after experiencing these deep tones?

Word Play

Scientists and biblical scholars have differing opinions on how our universe began. However, whether it's the spoken word of God or a "Big Bang," experts seem to agree it was some sort of sound. Thus, sound is very sacred.

How we talk to ourselves and to others is essential to our state of being.

Our bodies are always listening to our words. Therefore, I am also learning to speak to myself in a loving kind way.

Did you ever notice how similar the words "words" and "sword" are? Why is that?

Because words carry energetic vibrations.

We all understand how some words carry negative emotions. Some words are so offensive, we try to never use them.

Words can be swords, so be mindful of your choices. Are you going to uplift and heal yourself and others with your words? Or will you hurt and demean them with your swords?

Think about this: How many times a day does someone ask you how you are doing? What do you say?

Fine? Ok? Pretty good?

How does this feel?

Now try this:

When someone asks, "How are you doing today?," answer:

I am glorious!
I am magnificent!

Reflection

How does this feel?

Exercise: High Vibration Words

Circle one word from the list of words below.

All of these words carry a high vibration, meaning elevated levels of love and joy are associated with each word.

Whenever people use one of these words, they use it in a loving way. They use the words to offer kindness and love to another.

Lovely	Joyful
Enchanting	Spectacular
Delighted	Illuminating
Inspiring	Marvelous
Blissful	Breathtaking

Choose just one word today. Wherever you go, use this word. If no one asks you how you are feeling, just drop your word into a conversation.

Use this special word in all your emails, social media posts, and conversations throughout your day. Try to find a way to give others the gift of uplifting speech, too.

At the end of the day, think about how you feel after having used your special word all day.

Look at the list of words again.

Do you sense how words and positive intentions can change how you feel? Try adding a new word to your vocabulary each day. See how including these words in your conversations affects others and how it affects you.

Reflection

After a week, reflect on your word choices. Can you feel the difference between saying "I'm spectacular" versus saying, "I'm fine"?

Give yourself and those in your world the gift of these loving and affirming words every day!

Games People Play

Those blessed days of childhood - the time when (for most of us) our job is to play, to just be, and to giggle.

Take a moment and look back.

- What were your favorite games as a child?
- What did you love doing? What could you spend hours playing?
- What did you have fun imagining?

Take a little trip down memory lane.

Why is this so important? We all need a little time to play. Grief can be so heavy that sometimes it feels like our emotions are hanging on us like physical burdens.

Also, consider how many children are in the world. If every child in the world liked playing with dolls, where would our engineers come from? We all have varied interests for a reason.

I believe our hobbies hold the key to our sacred gifts and talents in this life.

Exercise: Fun activities I did in my youth

Make a list here of all those fun activities you did in your youth.

Here is my list:
1. Mom/House/Babies
2. Nurse
3. Kiddles/Fairies/Flowers
4. Books
5. Music and Dancing

Fun things I did when I was younger

Analyze your list. Can you find the adult equivalent of the fun things you did as a young person in your list of fun things you do as an adult? Ask for help if you are having trouble.

My list of fun things I do as an adult

1. Mom
I am currently a mom to three young adults. When I get the age they need me less, I'm going to hire myself out as a baby holder.

2. Nurse
I love helping others. As long as I continue to do this, I feel fulfilled.

3. Fairies
I've always been fascinated with the idea a little fairy lives inside flowers and fairies are best friends with the honey bees. I sometimes find myself looking at the bark of trees and imagining a tiny door exists or seeing flowers and thinking the fairies colored them brighter overnight.

To indulge my imaginative mind, I walk in the forest regularly....and see where my imagination takes me...

4. Books
I keep a pile of books by my bed so I can always be ready to read, or I can write a book!

5. Dancing
As a young child I loved music with dancing. I was a Zumba instructor for 8 years. I feel better after dancing. I feel lighter and more at ease in the world.

Exercise: The adult equivalent of fun things

Can we get your inner child to come out to play?

Adult equivalent of fun things I did when I was younger

Look at your list. Look at it again. Find one thing, just one that you can add into your day.

Make your play time a priority. Let your inner child shine and trust the call of the Divine to develop your gift and offer it to the world.

Sun Therapy

Have you ever noticed that when its sunny, you have more energy? Being in the sun feels good! When we were kids we knew this and playing outside was essential to our mental health. Animals understand this and voluntarily find ways to soak up the sun.

Today, find 15 minutes to experience some rays. If you are too busy or it's the middle of winter, pull over in a parking lot or crank open your window - just get some sun on your skin.

Allow the sun to wash over you and be willing to receive the warmth and healing energy. Know how vital the sun is to everyday life. It is essential to plants, trees, and our bodies. Bask in the warmth and reflect on three things you are grateful for.

Exercise: Gratitude
Write them down three things you are grateful for.

I am grateful for:
1.

2.

3.

Sit in the moment as long as you can and feel how truly blessed you are. Let your thoughts wander to the Creator.

Know this: the sun was created for YOU.

Exercise: A week of gratefulness

Do this every day for a week. Save your list here. How has your list changed over the past week?

Day	I'm grateful for:	I'm grateful for:	I'm grateful for:
Sunday			
Monday			
Tuesday			
Wednesday			
Thursday			
Friday			
Saturday			

Reflection on gratitude exercise

Random Act of Kindness

Mark died suddenly. He was never ill and there was no real warning. Pulmonary blood clots can do that. His passing left me feeling vulnerable and alone. It was like someone ripped off my blanket in sub-zero temperatures.

Other times, I struggled with feeling cursed. I felt like the Creator forgot about me and my children. Yet somehow, in the strangest ways, people from all walks of life (earth angels) stepped in to remind me there is goodness in the world.

How did these people, who were sometimes complete strangers, know I needed help? I can only imagine the divine orchestration that occurs in the next dimension of Heaven to aid humanity.

Exercise: Gratefulness

Write down three things you are grateful for. Keep this at home.

I am grateful for:

1.
2.
3.

Now, as you go about your day, pay attention to situations where you can make a difference. Even if it seems small, if an idea pops into your head, recognize it as coming from an Angel and act upon it. We don't necessarily know what part we may play in an angelic assistance plan.

Some examples are:
- Open the door for someone
- Bring someone coffee
- Let a fellow traveler cut in front of you
- Help someone move a heavy object
- Ask someone how they are and actually listen to their response
- Compliment someone on a piece of clothing or jewelry that stands out to you, and ask them about it

At the end of day, look back on your gratitude list.
- How do you feel?
- Any new insights?
- Does what you are grateful for change between the morning and now?
- Did anything you did for someone else change what you include in your gratitude list?
- Why do you think that is?
- How do you feel?
- Do you feel like you are part of a larger family?
- Does the term being in harmony with the world resonate with you?

Reflection on gratefulness

Dream On

Have you ever had a "visit" dream from your loved one? A dream so real and vivid you can still recall the words and the scenery and the emotions? In my experience, visit dreams feel as real as any waking memory. Such a dream is a gift from our loved one. I truly believe they can connect with us in our dream state.

Right before Mark's passing, I had an unusual dream. It was particularly real and symbolic. I knew it was important when it happened but didn't know why. In fact, it made such an impression on me that I wrote down details of the dream and even discussed the dream's possible significance with Mark.

In my dream, it was a sunny day. I was walking by myself up the hill towards my grandmother's house. About halfway up the hill, Mark pulled up in his blue car. He got out and we walked the rest of the way together.

When we reached Grandma's house, we stood outside the gate, and at that point, Mark disappeared. I took a step forward and opened the gate into Grandma's yard. My Grandma and Great Aunt Eva were on the other side of the gate. There was much hugging and happiness. The next thing that happened was Grandma handed me a baby girl. This baby girl was wearing pink and had dark hair with pigtails.

As soon as I started holding this baby girl, the whole scene changed. No longer was I in Grandma's yard, but I was at a party and we all were eating pizza.

To most people, this sounds like an ordinary dream. In reality, there are many truths and symbols woven into it that I'm still trying to decipher.

Let's break it down:

Walking uphill on a sunny day - this is a nice way to explain my life. My life has been sunny overall, with the typical uphill challenges we all have.

I was halfway up the hill when Mark drove up in his car. Mark entered my life easily. I started dating Mark when I was 22. Mark died when I was 44.

As I pass through the gate, I am greeted by my grandma and aunt. I now understand this to mean my future involves honoring the wisdom of women and children. Of note, they had both passed several years before this dream.

Grandma hands me a baby girl wearing pink. I believe the baby girl symbolized me. I need to come back into having childlike wonder and begin loving life. I'm starting my life again.

The dream becomes a pizza party. I haven't yet figured this out.

I love to analyze my dreams. It's like having a video library inside my head that is tailor made just for me.

Did you know that the ancients used to analyze their dreams? They believed they could find answers and guidance in their dreams.

Exercise: Asking for advice and clarifications

Write a list of things for which you would like some advice or clarification.

List of things for which I would like advice or clarification

- Before going to bed, select one item from your list. If you cannot pick just one, close your eyes and let your fingers choose a topic.
- Write it down on a piece of paper and put it under your pillow.
- Keep a paper and pencil by your bed so you can write down any ahas or insights you get during the night.
- Focus on the topic you selected.
- Close eyes ask your Spiritual advisor/Jesus/Guardian Angel to guide you while you are dreaming.
- Take some deep breaths.
- Close your eyes.
- Go to sleep.
- When you wake up, write down any dreams you can remember in as much detail as possible.

My Dreams

What is my first impression of the dream(s)?

What do you think your dream(s) mean?

Carry your notes (or this book) with you all day.

Your interpretation of your dream may change as you go through your day. Reflect on this and what caused any changes in your interpretation.

How my dream interpretation changed over the day.

Did you receive an answer to your question?

Make some notes on the answer and draw the first symbol that pops into your head.

The answer I received

The symbol

Baby Baby

After Mark died, I was often overwhelmed. My responsibilities quadrupled overnight and, as a result, my own physical health deteriorated. I now had to deal with all the family's financial worries and all the family responsibilities, as well as stomach issues, gallstones, food allergies, neck pain, etc. Some days the weight of my worries left me feeling as though I was being crushed into the earth.

One day, I came upon my baby picture. I'm about two years old in the photo and sitting with my dear siblings: my older sister (Mary) and brother (Mike). I'm so little that even though I am in a toddler chair, my feet do not touch the floor. It's a black and white picture and I love it. For some reason, I stuck this picture on my calendar.

Over time, when I felt stressed, my eyes would fall upon this picture. For a moment, I would take in the cuteness of that moment ~ me sitting and smiling with my siblings. After a while, I realized I NEEDED this reminder, this break in the constant stream of fear and worry. The message was clear: I needed to be gentle with myself and to take time to just be me.

I now like to look at this image of me and my siblings to remind me I'm lovable, and that I am doing the best I can. When I forget to take care of something (grief can affect your memory), I look at the photo and remember I'm only one person who has to be both Mom and Dad to my three children. That's enough for anyone.

I also use this picture as a reminder to care for myself. Just like a toddler, I give myself breaks from time to time. Grief can be so tiring. I may lay down in the middle of the day if I feel overwhelmed with the heavy emotions of loss. If I'm having a

hard moment, I reward myself with loving words and self-care like time in nature, massages, and essential oils.
I have learned to "husband" myself.

Exercise: Loving Your Baby Self

Do you have a baby picture of yourself? If you do, take it out and gaze at that sweet little version of you. If you don't have your baby picture, imagine yourself as an infant.
Notice where you are, who is with you, and appreciate your adorable face.

When I look at my baby picture, I see many things about myself.
- I am lovable just the way I am.
- I am precious.
- I am vulnerable.
- I am worthy.
- I am adorable.

Make a list of what you see about yourself in the photo

Now, put your baby picture and your list in a place where you will see them often - perhaps your desk, calendar, or computer monitor. Be strategic - use the place where you feel the most overwhelmed. Whenever you feel frustrated, look at your photo and list.

Reflection

Reflect on how you can love yourself today in the box below.
- What can you do to care for you today?
- What's the most kind and gentle action you take for yourself?
- What can you do in this very moment to ease some of your burdens?
- How can I be nice to myself today?

I've come to believe this is how our Creator sees all of us - perhaps small in our understandings of life, AND endlessly lovable.

What do you see when you look at a picture of yourself?

Missing You....

Who was your loved one on the inside?

What was your loved one's best quality?

What do you miss most about your loved one?

My late husband Mark was a gifted go-getter! He was the kind of guy who made life happen with his sheer will and magnetic personality. Mark had an incredible sense of humor. He could make brushing your teeth funny, and he often did!

Most days, the quality I miss most is his sense of humor.

Today's assignment is to make a list of your loved one's qualities and what you miss most about that person.

Take your time and dig deep.

Here is my list:

Best Qualities
1. Creativity
2. Drive

What I Miss Most
1. Humor

Use the workspace on the next page to list out your loved one's best qualities and what you miss most about that person.

My loved one's name:

_____'s best qualities

What I miss most about _____.:

After Mark passed, I noticed I often didn't smile for days at a time. Smiling felt weird. Smiling didn't fit into my new life - yet somehow smiling made me miss him more.

One day, my brilliant BFF (Michele) suggested I watch the tv show, "Modern Family." In case you have never seen it, it's a light hearted comedy whose characters tend to get funnier the longer you watch. After one episode, I was hooked. After that, I watched one or two funny shows per day. This became my new therapy.

I don't watch anything else on Netflix or TV. Ever. I have lived and survived enough shock and surprise to last a lifetime, so for

me 20-30 minutes of light comedy (my second favorite is
Wizards of Waverly Place!) is all I need.

I've learned to use comedy as a tool to help me relax and take
some of the weight off my shoulders. It's been said that
laughter is the best medicine and I have to agree.

Now, look at your list again and see if we can figure out a way to
bring some elements of the qualities of your loved one that you
so desperately miss into your new life.

Do you miss your loved one's closeness or touch? Consider
having a monthly massage or even weekly sessions at a massage
school. Was your loved one your best friend? Did he/she
understand you better than anyone? Try joining a grief support
group. A grief support group is a great way to connect with
people who are sharing your experience. Keep searching for the
right group until you find one that suits your personality.
Was your loved one an awesome listener? Consider finding a
new mode for expressing yourself. Explore journaling, painting,
creating. There are lots of ways to express yourself. You could
even write a book!

Ask others for help and support. Understand that love is all
around us - we just need to make space to receive it

This last paragraph is for the serious-minded only; the ones who
have had enough of this new life and are willing to do
ANYTHING to feel better....

Are you ready?

TAKE ON one of your beloved's qualities. BE like her or him.
Branch out, grow some wings, and FLY. You've survived the
worst already and probably amazed even yourself. You have the
power to choose your life. What would happen if you chose to
be like your loved one?

You can be courageous.

My choice is that I'm taking an absolute leap of faith by writing this book and having a website. I've always worked in the medical field. However, by being "entrepreneurial" like my late husband, I can relate even more to him.

I see now how hard it must have been for him to always be creating. I understand some of the uncertainty and fear he must have felt. I've received a tiny piece of him post mortem that I never knew I could find and that helps to ease the pain of him being gone.

Reflection

- Can you incorporate one of your loved one's best qualities into your life?
- Can you spread your wings a little and fly?
- What do you see now?
- Better yet~ how do you feel?
- What do you choose?

Sunset

Find out when the sun goes down in your area and go to a place where you can watch it for at least 15 minutes. Remember that the time of sunset changes throughout the year, especially as you move further from the equator, so double-check the time before you go.

Exercise: Reflect on your day.

As you watch the sunset, think back over your day.

- What are you grateful for?
- Who loves you?
- Expand your scope.
- Who else loves you?
- Friends?
- Co-workers?
- Neighbors?
- Church/Club members who are always there for you?
- Can you sense the many ways nature supports and loves you?
- Who do you love?

Now, look back to when your loved one was alive.

- Have your perceptions of how others feel about you changed since your loved one's passing?
- Is your understanding of the role nature plays in your life different?

Reflect on these questions in the workspace on the next page.

Reflection on your day

Part 3: CPR Exercises

Do you know you?

Have you ever done a Myers Briggs Personality assessment?

Yes? Then, how about the Strengths Finder assessment?

Find a personality assessment you haven't done and spend 10-15 minutes doing it.

What do you see when you look at your results? You're pretty amazing, right?

Let's look. Is there a quality or gift you haven't been using lately? Let's show it off!

Exercise: My Top 5 Qualities

Make a list of the top five qualities you identified in the assessment and put it next to your phone or your bed to remind yourself how amazing you are.

My Top 5 Qualities

1.
2.
3.
4.
5.

Try working your best qualities into conversations with others and so both of you can fall in love with YOU!

103
Part 3: CPR Exercises

Love Me More

The hardest part of Mark's passing was losing the feeling of his ever-loving presence surrounding and protecting me on a daily basis. When he died, I felt like someone ripped my warm winter coat from my body and left me standing alone one bitterly cold dark January night.

At some point, I realized I hadn't been using the word love in any context. I stopped saying things like "I love this book or I love your new haircut." I had erased the word love from my vocabulary and my reality.

Most days, I felt like I was watching the world from my TV screen. I was never in the action - I was always on the periphery and always alone.

Eventually the tears dried, but I just felt hollow.

Something had to change. So I changed me.

I began the process of listening and tuning into my body. Our bodies are ALWAYS trying to get our attention, but most of the time we ignore our own personal medical alert system.

No one talks about how much grief hurts physically. I remember the aching and feeling of despair in my muscles. It was so deep I thought it would never go away.

I began to have deep tissue massages. This helped me to feel a sense of normalcy in my body and I often went as often as every two weeks.

Maybe I was just missing human contact. Maybe I was lonely for touch.

Reflection

- What is your body telling you?
- What hurts or aches?

Practice

- Go to a quiet place where you will not be disturbed.
- Breathe deeply in and out.
- Discuss with your Spiritual guide, Jesus, or your Guardian Angel how you want to feel and ask for help.
- Close your eyes, and starting with your feet, focus on each area of your body.

What is your body telling you?

- How does it feel?
- Listen and wait... does a word or feeling pop into your head as you concentrate?

Using the diagram on the next page, write down the emotion(s) you sense for each area of your body. If you do not receive an answer readily, move on to the next part of your body. Keep in mind that you may not receive an emotion for each area.

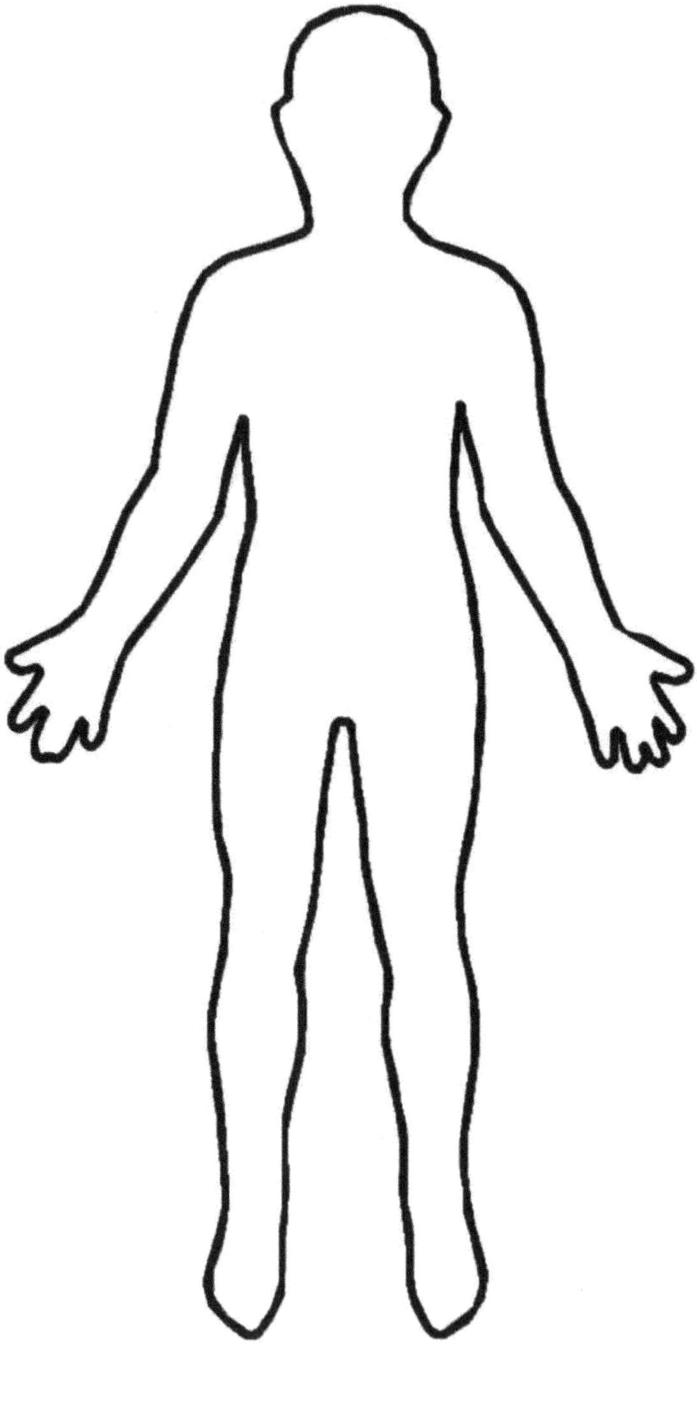

Now, create a list of the emotions and feelings you noticed for each area of your body.

Body Part	Emotions and Feelings
Head	
Face	
Throat	
Shoulders	
Arms	
Hands	
Chest	
Heart	
Stomach	
Buttocks	
Thighs	
Calves	
Feet	
Anything else	

I describe two different ways to use this list of emotions below. Experiment with each method and find what suits you or, even better, develop your own way to listen and interpret your body's personal communication.

Remember that we are not our feelings.

How many times have you said, "I am sad" or "I am angry"?

Perhaps a kinder way to understand this is to say, "I am feeling sad." We can always change our feelings.

Method # 1
- After you have scanned your body and compiled a list of areas that require attention, I invite you again to close your eyes.
- Focus on your breathing and bring yourself to a relaxed state.
- Hold your hands out in front of you and ask your Heavenly Creator or Jesus to send healing into your hands.
- You might feel a heating sensation or warmth.
- Some of you may not feel anything at all and that is perfectly acceptable.
- Now place your hands on those body parts that need attention.
- If you intuitively receive the message that an area needs massage, stretching, or a particular movement, follow this guidance.
- Spend as much as you think is necessary to administer your special medicine.

Method # 2
- Begin again with your list.
- Breathe deeply and slowly until you feel relaxed.

- Ask Jesus or your spiritual advisor for assistance.
- Using your list, send your loving intention and breath to specific areas of discomfort.
- Depending on what emotions your body holds, consider sending love, healing, or compassion.
- For example, if you experience sadness in your heart, as you take a deep breath, say in your mind, "I'm breathing love in to my heart."
- As you exhale, say in your mind, "I'm breathing out all my sadness."

Repeat this process at least three times for each affected area of your body.

Other examples:
- When you breathe in, say, "I'm breathing in compassion to my aching neck" and as you exhale, say, "I'm breathing out my loneliness."

- When you breathe in, say, "I'm breathing in healing to my stomach," and as you exhale, say, "I'm letting go of my anger over expectations."

I like to start each day with a body scan to see where trapped emotions may lay. I now trust my body is here to help me and I no longer fear my body's discomfort. I understand now my body is trying to help me.

Try to spend a week doing each method I described above, and then determine what works for you and feels best to you physically.

Honor the wisdom of your body.

Of note, I also found reading Louise Hay's book, "You Can Heal Your Life" to be very enlightening.

Lipstick and Mirrors

Loving yourself is one of the most important things you will do in your life.

Self-love changes and expands everything - our thoughts, the people in our lives, the choices we make, our interactions with others, and our expectations of ourselves and others.

When we lose someone we love, we sometimes shut our hearts down in fear of being hurt again, but love is the only way to feel good again.

Our core essence is love.

Exercise: Self Love

- Go to the place you look at yourself most – perhaps your bathroom mirror.
- Look in the mirror.
- Look past the physical you.
- Look deeply in your eyes.
- See the amazing survivor and thriver who dwells within your body.
- Now, draw a heart on your mirror.
- Place your hands over your physical heart.
- Breathe slowly in and out.
- Every time you walk by the heart on the mirror, look at yourself deeply and say,
- "I love me.
- I love ME
- I LOVE ME."

Do this every day until you really and truly believe it.

Candle Rx

Sometimes, when we suffer major losses, our faith in the divine is shaken. We may feel cursed, cheated, ignored, betrayed - so many different emotions.

It's hard to make sense of it all.

But trying to be logical may not be the way to process grief.

After all, grief is not a cognitive function, it is an emotion – something that is felt.

So, it makes sense that the way to ease grief is by connecting with our senses.

Exercise: Write a letter
- Write a letter to Jesus or your Heavenly Creator.
- Explain how you feel within your heart right now.
- Include how you want to feel.
- Be specific.
- Say everything you need to say.
- Now, go somewhere quiet/private. Night is often a good time for this exercise.
- Light a candle.
- Sit comfortably.
- Take three deep breaths.
- Ask your Spiritual advisor, Jesus, or Angels to be present.
- Take some time to watch the candle.
- Notice the flame and how it flickers, and changes.
- Breathe in the scent of the candle.
- Place a hand on your heart.
- Tell your Jesus or your Spiritual Advisor you would like to speak from your heart.
- Ask that your heart be connected to their heart.

- Feel this.
- Take three more deep breaths.
- Now, read your letter out loud.
- Read it slowly, pausing for emphasis.
- Allow any tears to fall as they may.
- Read until you are done.
- Ask Jesus/Heavenly Creator to guide you and turn your attention back to the flickering candle.
- Receive and be open to the messages that come immediately and over the next few days.
- Keep this letter.

Reflection

How do you feel now?

Check back one week later, would you write the same letter today? Why? What has changed?

Kitchen Duty

The finality of death means we don't always get to end the relationship the way we would have wanted. There may be words left unspoken or unresolved misunderstandings.

One top of this, deaths can (especially in the case of a spouse) leave us with more responsibilities and less time and capacity to manage them.

Since Mark's unexpected death, I've had chronic neck pain. Frequent massages, chiropractic visits, and orthotics became a part of my life. All were helpful, but none ever completely alleviated the pain.

Last spring I found myself in a 1.5 hour bus ride to the mountains in Australia with my two daughters. I had a crushing migraine. Luckily, I had medication for this in my purse and for the next hour or so, I listened to meditation music to lower the intense pain.

I must have drifted off to sleep and had some type of out of body experience. I was somehow back home in my kitchen. My dad knocked on the door (he had been gone for ten years by this time) and came in.

I went through some sort of forgiveness prayer with him. I am sorry, please forgive me, I love you, I forgive you for ____, please forgive me for _____, and it's time for you to go. I had read about the Hawaiian forgiveness prayer of Ho ʻoponopono and parts of it must have drifted into my head at this moment.

Dad came in one door one the left and went out another door on the right. After this, a whole stream of people showed up: Mark, Maddie, Sam, Kate, other family, and so on. I had something to say to everyone. Some of the people seemed to give me messages, too. I dozed off and when I woke up we were in the mountains.

The weird thing is my neck pain and headache were completely gone. I guess I'd been carrying around a lot of unspoken emotions.

My challenge for you:

- Rate your pain on a scale of one to ten
- Take a few deep breaths
- Close your eyes and breathe deeply
- Call in your Spiritual Advisor, Jesus, or your Guardian Angels.
- Envision yourself standing in a room with two doorways.
- The doorway to the left is for new people who arrive.
- The doorway to the right is for people to leave.
- Ask your Angels for help in removing any stored-up resentment.
- Ask for help in identifying people you need to forgive or ones you may have tried to offer an apology.
- Close your eyes.
- Who pops into your mind?
- What messages come in?
- Symbols?
- Emotions?

- After you have received messages from everyone, check on your pain level.
- Do you have less pain?
- What is different?
- How do you feel?

Reflection

Write down whatever comes to you as you reflect on the questions on the previous page.

Bathing with Roses

My late husband gave me many compliments. He often told me I was as beautiful on the inside as I was on the outside. Mark admired my intuitive perception and asked for advice often. After death, life became eerily still and it wasn't always easy to remember those loving words.

Some days I forget I was once loved and cherished.

When you have difficult moments do you say unkind things to yourself? Have you ever forgotten who you really are?

Here are some of the ugly words I've heard bouncing around in my head:
- Why did you do that?
- Stop crying!
- You never do anything right!

Reflection

Make a list of the unkind words you've said to yourself.

Exercise: Loving Thoughts

- Purchase a single rose from the store.
- Draw a bath.
- Add sea salt or Epsom salts.
- Light several candles.
- Say a special prayer request and ask Jesus, your Spiritual Advisor, or Guardian Angels to be with you in this moment.
- Step into the bath with your rose.
- Imagine you are being cradled in love.
- Close your eyes and breathe in the warmth of the water and the scent of the sea salts.
- Who is holding you?
- Is it your spouse or perhaps Jesus or your guardian Angel?
- What do you feel? Trust what you feel. Don't overthink it.
- Ask Jesus or your Spiritual advisor to help rid you of this need to be unkind to yourself.
- Take one leaf from the stem of the flower and drop in into the water and say instead of_____, I'm going to say_____ and listen for guidance.
- Do this slowly and deliberately for the five or six criticisms you have of yourself.
- Next look at all the beautiful petals on the rose. Each petal represents a special part of YOU.
- Listen for the loving thoughts that are coming from your Angelic guides and each time you are reminded of one of your special qualities, place a petal on your body.
- I am loved
- I am enough
- I am worthy
- I am courageous
- Lay covered in rose petals and soak in the warmth.
- Feel the outpouring of celestial caring.
- Know you are supported and held in love always.
- As you watch the water go down the drain, release and let go of all your self-criticism.

Reflection

What did you experience during this exercise?

Part 3: CPR Exercises

Fun / Free

After we lose someone, our social circle may change. We may not feel the same. The bonds that kept us in a particular group may be altered or we may change where we live. Our social circle may change for any number of reasons

Today, look in your community paper or online sources to find free things to do this weekend. For example, "Open Door Milwaukee" happens every autumn. It's totally free, and on these special days you have access to free tours and unique places you could not normally see.

The reason this is so special is sometimes us grieving folks like to shut down. We like to go to the same places and do the same activities just to feel safe. We find comfort in the familiar.

However, we are not the same people as we were before the deaths of our loved ones. We are survivors and as such we have had to do many things outside our comfort zones. We have expanded and there are new parts of us waiting to be birthed and born.

So, let's honor that new creation, that new you.

- Go to free concerts.

- Go to free lectures at your local library.

- Go to a free play in a park.

- Go to a free museum to take in the beautiful art.

It's amazing what you can do on a shoestring and how revitalizing these fresh new experiences can be!

Reflection

What free activity did you do today? What impact did it have on you?

Birds & Butterflies

Have you had any unusual experiences with birds, butterflies, or any other animal since your loved one's death?

I have. Let me explain.

My dad died from cancer in July of 2007. About three days after his passing, I found myself sitting outside on our deck one beautiful sunny morning with my three children. We were all in a sad, reflective state of mind. My daughter Maddie, who was 11 at the time, was retelling a vivid dream she had the night before about her grandfather.

A few minutes later, the most extraordinary thing happened. Seemingly out of nowhere, a black and royal blue butterfly began to fly around us. I had never seen a butterfly like this is in our state!

After a minute or so it swooped down and landed on Maddie's left hand - her ring finger to be exact.

We all just sat there, not quite realizing what we were seeing, just watching the butterfly in awe - then after a minute or two, the butterfly flew away.

I looked around the yard and didn't see it anymore. It was as if it disappeared.

Time passed and my grief over Dad's passing dissipated. I knew he lived a full and wonderful life and I was at peace.

However, a year later I found myself sad once again after attending Father's Day mass. There was something about the songs and thinking about how much Dad loved being an usher at church. I came home and walked outside onto my deck and then called my sweet sister Tricia to commiserate. As we talked, I was visited by a black and blue butterfly! The EXACT same unique flying beauty, and once again, it swooped and swirled around me and then flew away.

To this day, those are the ONLY two times I have ever seen a butterfly of this particular color. I have researched this a bit, and the closest butterfly I can find is the MALE spicebush swallowtail, which is typically found in the South. THEY DON'T LIVE IN WISCONSIN!

This was a gift of reassurance from my dad. I have no doubt.

Now, imagine for a moment what it might be like for our loved ones after they pass. Their love for us is eternal. However, they cannot speak to us as they used to. It's like they're stuck behind a soundproof glass window. I believe they can see us but cannot interact with us. Perhaps, the only way they can communicate with us is by influencing the energy of animals or birds here on earth.

What better way to signal they have ascended into the higher realms or heaven than by getting our attention via a bird or butterfly?

Please note, I'm not suggesting your loved one has turned into a bird or butterfly or some other animal! I am merely hypothesizing that since everyone and everything is energy, is it possible our loved ones can connect to the energy of the Earth via a bird or butterfly in an attempt to comfort us?

I say YES! What do you think?

Since your loved one's passing, have you experienced any atypical encounters with winged creatures or animals?

Reflection

- What was the message?
- How did you feel?
- Do you believe in your heart they were a messenger from your loved one?

Angelic Whispers...

Believe it or not, we have all had Angels speak to us. It may not sound like trumpets or a flutter of wings. Sometimes, if we are paying attention, we just might hear the most perfect words of advice from a seemingly complete stranger. Or, a random license plate gives us the exact message we have been seeking. That's your Angels helping to create a feeling of love and caring for you every day and everywhere you go!

One day, a few years after my husband Mark's passing, I was really struggling. Every parent of teenage children can relate to this - there comes a time when your wonderful kids are suddenly rude and disrespectful. You cannot believe they are the same sweet children who used to eagerly sit on your lap and read bedtime stories!

I had a really awful moment like this once. I'm not one who cries easily about the unfairness of my current situation, but this moment overwhelmed me. I felt beat down and tired and defeated. The next thing I knew, I was bending over to pick a sock up off the floor when an Angel leaned in and whispered into my ear.

In an instant, an old familiar song "poured" into my left ear. It was a song from long ago that I hadn't thought about in probably 30 or more years! A song so obscure, but oh so perfect, for the situation. A song I could not recall the lyrics to if asked...

"Who can turn the world on with her smile?
Who can take a nothing day and suddenly make it all seem
worthwhile...
Well it's you girl, and you should know it...
With each glance and every little moment you show it

Love is all around, no need to waste it
You can have the town, why don't you take it..

You're going to make it after all....
You're going to make it after all!!!!"

It was the theme from the Mary Tyler Moore Show.

I KNEW this was from above.
I KNOW this was to remind me that I was loved and not to despair.
I BELIEVE absolutely this was a gift and I gratefully received it.

Have you ever had an unexpected song or idea "pop" or "drop" into your head?

Has the most perfect song come on the radio as if for your ears only?

How did it make you feel?

Reflect and receive.

Part 3: CPR Exercises

Here Comes the Sun

I clearly remember what it was like waking up for the first few months after Mark died. I would slowly come out of my dream state in response to the ringing of my alarm and then, like a hammer, the knowledge he was gone would hit me all over again.

Does this happen to you?

Do you want to change your perspective?

Exercise: Gratitude at Sunrise

- Make a plan to get up early tomorrow and watch the sunrise. Be sure to bring a pad of paper and a pen.
- Find a spot with a view. As you watch the sun rise, make a list of everything you are grateful for.
- List EVERYTHING for which you are grateful. Everything - from having shoes to wear to owning a pen to write with.

I am grateful for:

At the end of the day, check in with yourself.
- How do you feel?
- Do you feel any different?
- Why?

End of day check in

Now make another list. This time reflect on your blessings throughout the day.

Today's blessings

Are you more aware of your blessings?

Reflection on being aware of your blessings

Mary, Mary, Quite Contrary

My "always loved to tease me" dad passed away in 2007 from kidney cancer. He was 77 and had lived a wonderful, fulfilling life. Afterwards, many of us in the family experienced what I like to call "visit" dreams or received significant signs we knew for sure came from him. However, Mom didn't receive any visits and this added to her suffering.

So, I attempted to do what Mom did in times of need. I said a novena for her. I asked for Mom to receive a definite sign or dream as a clear message from Dad.

I did this daily for weeks, and the most extraordinary thing happened one morning. I woke up from a vivid dream. In this dream, Dad was alive and sitting up and my whole family was around. It was very real and so happy.

I felt like I really needed to share how incredible this all was so I called my younger sister Tricia.

I began to tell her about my dream. After about the third sentence she began screaming with excitement. She had the exact same dream the night before, too!

My heart fluttered and my arms and legs began to tingle with goosebumps. This was not a coincidence!

I received this as a blessing and an answer to my novena. I also realized that although my intention was for Mom to receive a sign, it was nonetheless an absolute gift from heaven for me.

Divine timing does not adhere to earthly standards. Perhaps this was something I needed to learn.

Reflection
- Have you ever asked for help in a particular situation?
- What kind of heavenly guidance did you receive?
- Was it what you asked for?
- Was it helpful in some way?

Consider doing a daily novena for a problem you cannot solve. A novena is a Catholic prayer practice said over 9 days or 9 hours at a consistent time, such as 11 am for a 9-day practice or 15 minutes after the hour for a 9-hour practice. The novena tradition goes back to the time of the Apostles. The prayer is a request for special grace and many believe a novena connects with God's ears directly.

How to do a novena:

- Write out a request for what you need.
- Refer back to this request before each novena.
- After the nine days or hours have passed, look back at your request - has anything changed?

Example:
Novena to the Infant Jesus of Prague

O Jesus,
Who has said, "ask and you shall receive, seek and you shall
find, knock and it shall be opened," through the intercession of
Mary, Your most holy Mother, I knock, I seek, I ask that my
prayer be granted.

(State your request)

O Jesus
Who has said, "all that you ask of the Father in My Name, He
will grant you," through the intercession of Mary Your Most Holy
Mother, I humbly and urgently ask your Father in your name
that my prayer be granted.

(State your request)

O Jesus
Who has said, "Heaven and earth shall pass away but my word
shall not pass away," through the intercession of Mary your
Most Holy Mother, I feel confident that my prayer will be
granted.

(State your request)

Note: You don't have to be Catholic to say a novena.

Puppy Love

Losing Mark created an enormous hole in my life and in our family. Some days this loss felt like a crater too big to pass through and too deep to see the bottom of.

Through the many heartbreaking days, a special little hero remained a constant light in the darkness of our lives. I'm talking about our family dog, Champ.

Champ was a 25-pound Teddy Bear (Bichon Frise/Shih Tzu mix) who bounced into our lives for Christmas of 2006. He wasn't just a dog; he was part of the family with an old soul. Champ was a friend to everyone.

In many ways, he was the glue that held our family together. Champ always knew when someone was sick or just needed some company. With his soft brown eyes he said everything our hurting hearts needed to hear.

During the long surreal days of that summer in 2010, I often took the kids to a place of magic: Green Meadows petting farm in Burlington, Wisconsin. Mavis and the staff offered a special place with animals of all sorts to meet and interact with.

Holding baby kittens, feeding chickens, and petting ponies became a new pastime. Watching baby goats play rivals any form of therapy in my book!

During these moments, for just a little while, we could lay down the burden of our sadness and just enjoy the wonder of creation.

When we look deeply into the eyes of an animal, we sense more than just the physical. In this moment, our souls meet and we communicate love to one another. If we are lucky, we get the opportunity to tell each other our stories.

Sadly, in 2016, our beloved Champ died. He taught us many things, but what stands out the most was how love doesn't always need words.

Reflection

- Do you know people who share their love without words?
- Do you have a pet? What do they "say" to you?
- If you don't have a pet, try one of the following.
- Observe someone else's dog or cat before doing this reflection.
- Offer to dog or cat sit.
- Spend time at an animal shelter.
- Observe wildlife through a window.
- Invest in a bird feeder.
- What do you notice?
- How do the people who love you show their feelings?
- How does spending time with them make you feel?

For me, there are many ways to experience Our Heavenly Creator, and the love and devotion one receives from a family pet is one of them.

Squirrels Speak

One morning, about a year or so after Mark died, I heard a very peculiar sound. It was quite noticeable because I was alone and all my children were at school.

I looked through the whole house, trying to find the source and eventually my search led me outside.

As I walked around my yard, I came upon a squirrel high up in the tree on my deck. I have a beautiful deck that is built around the tree. The poor little squirrel appeared to be wailing. It was not a sound I had never heard before.

I quickly searched for signs of an attack or even bloody footprints. There were none.

Somewhat mystified, I then went upstairs so I could view better from my bedroom window. As it was late fall, there were no leaves left on the tree and I could see it easily.

The squirrel seemed to be in distress. I couldn't detect any signs of injury. Was it rabid? I searched online for answers, but nothing seemed to fit.

Later I got into my car to go to an appointment. As I began to drive away, I saw, here, right in front of my house, was a freshly killed squirrel.

Could this wailing squirrel outside my window be the grieving mate?

This quickly brought me to tears and the cries of the squirrel haunted me for some days to come.

I then considered the possibility that this might be a message from beyond.

Of all the many trees around my house to use as a place to grieve, how did this squirrel decide on the tree literally right outside my bedroom window?

Was there more to this story?

My inquiring mind led me to Ted Andrews, author of "Animal Speak." In this book, he explores the Native American tradition of listening to the messages animals bring us. Paying attention to unusual experiences with animals may hold a message if you are open to understanding the lines of communication.

The author invites the reader to remember animal interactions and then look at the corresponding animal totem for possible guidance.

The squirrel animal totem is all about taking time out to have more fun and not to take life too seriously. Other messages from this totem involve simple repairs around the house.

I was completely blown away. This was so fitting for where I was in my life!

I definitely needed a reminder to have fun and, yes, my home needed some love!

Reflection

- Have you had any interesting encounters with animals or insects lately?
- Take a moment and think of a time now or around the time of your loved one's passing - did an animal seem to act differently around you?
- Did the animal make eye contact?

- Have you seen an animal in your dreams recently?
- Have any animals crossed your path?
- Is there an animal you are particularly drawn to?
- Next, I invite you to do a web search for this animal. Look for "animal spirit guides" or "animal totems."

What messages are the animals trying to send you?

Christmas in July

Do you like Christmas songs?

I do!

I often play them while working out or doing housework.

One day, I was listening to a song by Avalon called, "Light a Candle" and I was completely humbled. Tears came to my eyes as I considered all the people who helped me along the way on this new journey in my life - my life as a widow.

I could have given up many times, and I didn't because of all the kindness I received.

Being on the receiving end has taught me to look at the world in a different way.

I have learned little things do mean a lot.

I now know that when you have an impulse to help someone, how important it is to actually follow through and do it. You may be the reason they have a smile on their face when their children come home that day.

We never know how close someone is to breaking. When you listen to the little voice inside you, you might be the answer to someone else's prayers.

At first, the kindness I received was loving support at the funeral. Then it was meal assistance. Next came carpooling, and then the extraordinary acts of good will that seemed to occur just when I needed them most.

I am so grateful.

Exercise

- Listen to the song, "Light a Candle."
- Light a candle and close your eyes.
- Place your hands on your heart and reflect on the ordinary miracles and earth Angels in your life.
- Fill your heart with love and send this love back into the world and to all your helpers.
- How are you different since you lost your beloved?
- Do any intuitive thoughts come to mind?
- Is there someone who might need you to be an Earth Angel for today?

Reflection

"Light a Candle" lyrics

Light a candle
for the old man who sits staring
out a frosty window pane.

Light a candle
for the woman who is lonely
and every Christmas it's the same.

For the children who need
more than presents can bring.

Light a candle
Light the dark
Light the world
Light a heart or two
Light a candle for me
I'll light a candle for you

Light a candle
for the homeless and the hungry;
a little shelter from the cold.

Light a candle
for the broken and forgotten;
may the season warm their souls.

Can we open our hearts
to shine through the dark.

Light a candle
Light the dark
Light the world
Light a heart or two
Light a candle for me

I'll light a candle for you

And in this special time of year
may peace on Earth surround us here,
and teach us there's a better way to live.

Oh, and with every flame that burns,
we must somehow learn
that love's the greatest gift
that we could ever give.

Light a candle
Light the dark
Light the world
Light a heart or two
Light a candle for me
I'll light a candle for you.

Water World

Some days are just difficult. Grief is like that. You look around at your new reality and it still doesn't feel comfortable.

Maybe it's the extra responsibilities you carry, or perhaps it's harder to feel carefree and joyful on the many days you miss your loved one.

I had one of these days once while glancing through Facebook.

On this particular day, everyone seemed to be going on with their lives in the most enjoyable ways and I seemed to be standing still.

As luck would have it, an interesting post came across my feed about a doctor from Japan named Dr. Masaru Emoto, author of "The Hidden Messages in Water."

Dr Emoto conducted water experiments and found that exposing the water to positive words, music, and intentions impacted it in a highly beneficial way.

The pictures of water treated with loving words and intentions are absolutely beautiful.

The pictures of water exposed to harsh words and criticism showed jagged and irregular patterns in the water crystals.

The nurse inside me became completely intrigued. I knew that our bodies are made of approximately 65-70% water.

Reflection

What would happen if I started talking to and loving the water in my body? How would I feel?

How would my body feel if I blessed and appreciated the water before I drank it?

I know most people express appreciation for the food before they eat it, but how many people consider thanking and blessing their water? How many people actually talk to the water in their body?

Exercise: Talk to your body

● Look up Dr Emoto's water experiments and view the pictures for yourself.
● Fill in the blanks:

Most days I feel
The word that best describes me is
I am grateful for

● Set aside 2-3 times per day to spend time talking to your body.

A good practice is to talk with your body first thing in the morning, at midday, and when you go to bed. Another easy way is to do it at meal times.

Every time you drink water, speak to it as you would an old friend.
● Thank you, water.

● I am so grateful for you.

● You are amazing.

Return to this exercise one week later and fill in the blanks again.

| Most days I feel |
| The word that best describes me is |
| I am grateful for |

Reflection

Do you complete the statements in the same way?

Today

Today is a new day.

Today is the first day of the rest of your story.

Today is a great day to love yourself anew.

Ready?

Practice: How can I love myself today?

- Find yourself a comfortable place.
- Have a pen and pad of paper handy.
- Close your eyes.
- Breathe deeply in and out several times.
- Ask Jesus or your heavenly Creator for guidance.
- Place your hands on your heart.
- Ask yourself, "How can I love my body the most today?" Wait for an intuitive answer. I usually hear suggestions to drink more water.
- Next ask, "How can I honor my soul today?" I often hear ideas to spend more time alone
- Now ask yourself, "How can I heal my mind today?" Typically I hear recommendations to clean and clear areas of my house.

Do this practice every morning for a week.

Use the workspace on the next page to reflect how you feel.

Reflection

How do you feel?

Star Light Phone Call

My love passed so suddenly. He was just gone. It was July 2, 2010. Everyone else was celebrating. The day included barbecues, picnics, and sunshine, with neighborhood fireworks displays at night. We had planned to go to Summerfest, a large music festival, later that day.

The morning started out normal. We had coffee as we usually did while he got ready to go to work. Mark abruptly went to lay down because he didn't feel well. Not five minutes later I found myself calling 911.

I don't know how, but Mark knew he was dying. He was able to say a few words and he told me he would love me forever. And that's a gift I will hold deep in my heart always. Sadly, there wasn't time for advice on our children, exchange of computer passwords, or discussions of regrets.

Time has passed, but my need to communicate with Mark hasn't. My children still need a father, and I can only do my best. I still have questions.

Do you ever wish you could just pick up the phone and talk to your loved one? What if your loved one is trying to reach out to you as well? Do you wonder how you might be able to communicate?

Exercise – Celestial Telephone

- Wait for a clear night.
- At nightfall, walk outside and breathe deeply.
- Breathe in through your nose and out your mouth or nose slowly.
- Do this 3 times.

- Take in the beauty of the night
- Slowly scan the sky.
- Does one star catch your attention? Does it twinkle and sparkle just for you? Focus on that star.
- Close your eyes and imagine a phone.
- Ask Jesus or your spiritual guide for divine white protection and healing light.
- Ask for Jesus or your Spiritual guide's help in connecting with your loved one.
- Picture yourself scrolling down the contact list. Whose name does your hand stop on?
- Now open your eyes and focus on your star.
- What if your loved one in Heaven can also see the star you are looking at? Imagine what this would be like.
- Think of the star as your own personal celestial messenger.
- Talk to the star as if it is sending your message to your loved one.
- Say what you need to say.
- Pause...
- Do any insights pop in your head?
- Do you feel any physical sensations?
- Do you feel anything on the top of your head?
- Maybe it feels like a feather touching you or you sense a whisper of a touch.
- Take a few steps closer to the star.
- Open your arms.
- Take a few steps closer and open your arms again.
- Don't think, just feel and notice any emotions and memories that surface.
- When you have expressed all you need to, thank Jesus and your spiritual guides for protection and guidance.

Reflection

Were you able to connect? What was your loved one's message for you?

Sail Away

I used to think that grief was a linear journey. Or perhaps a sad game of hopscotch. Only when I completed a stage could I advance by jumping onto the next one.

Now I know it to be more like sailing.

Some days the sun shines and the waters are calm. I know where I am going and I am enjoying the ride.

Other days the waters are turbulent and stormy and I cannot see my way home. I feel lost and alone.

One way I navigate on these rough days is to strengthen my sailing vessel or my body.

How?

Exercise: Strengthening Your Vessel

- Find a quiet place
- Put on some soothing music
- Ask Jesus or your spiritual guide to be present
- Breath slowly and deeply
- Place one hand on your heart and reflect on all your blessings... what are you grateful for?
- After a while place your other hand on your heart ... think about all the people you love, including yourself. Let in a stream of love and just breathe ...

Remember to be grateful and loving to yourself for all you have been through, too!!

Now your heart is filled with love and gratitude.

Let's begin to improve your vessel even more.

- Rub your hands together.
- My dear friend Kim taught me to rub my hands together vigorously when I want to bring healing into my hands
- Ask Jesus or your spiritual guide to assist with healing
- Place your hands on your forehead to soothe your worries.
- Breathe slowly and deeply
- Do this until your worries subside
- Rub your hands together again and place them on your heart
- Continue to breathe deeply until your sadness lessens
- Rub your hands together and place them on your abdomen
- Breathe slowly
- Keep your hands there until your fears are eased
- Address any other areas that need healing
- Fill yourself with love, gratitude, and grace

During the worst storms in our lives, the sun (Jesus or Heavenly Creator) is still shining and waiting behind the clouds. The sun never stops shining.

Keep your vessel strong and you can feel that warmth through the darkest days

Reflection

What did you experience during the exercises?

Conclusion

Here is one way to view recovery from grief:

When an egg is broken by outside forces, the chick inside dies. However, if the chick inside initiates the process and slowly works and chips away at the interior of the egg, life begins. Thus, like a baby chick hatching from an egg, recovery from grief is best done from the inside.

My hope is for you to enjoy the outer to inner journey by coming home to your heart.

Please remember to always keep your cup of compassion full and spilling over so that there is enough for you to give to yourself and others. You are worthy of your love!

Take charge of your present time. It is a present waiting for you to unwrap. Combine your senses, your voice, and your body's rhythms with your intention for healing to keep you in the present.

Receive your loved one's messages through the spiritual realm. Receive the love of our Heavenly Creator in all of creation. Surrender to the knowing you are loved and share your heart light with the world.

I'd like to share one last memory with you.

My first birthday after Mark died was completely awful. I missed him badly and all I wanted was for him to come home, wrap his loving arms around me, and tell me everything was going to be OK again. Nothing felt right and no one could have done anything to make me feel better.

When I got the mail that day, I had an envelope from an unknown charity asking for donations. Inside was a pale pink rosary with tiny hearts. I thought it was quite pretty, put it aside, and then promptly forgot about it.

The next year on my birthday I felt better in some ways but the ache was almost worse because I didn't love my new reality and I didn't know how to begin creating a reality I loved.

I clearly remember getting up early, sitting at my kitchen counter, and looking out onto my deck, when I noticed something peculiar.

Inside a heart-shaped planter I received years before from my wonderful mother-in-law, Pat, was a sight to behold.

The planter looked neglected because I hadn't planted anything in it since the previous May, just before Marks passing. In fact the old dead plant was still inside.

Yet, that's where the miracle was - somehow, without any planting or watering by me, a small perfect sunflower had sprouted, grown, and bloomed!!

This was shocking! It blew open the doors to my heart and to many possibilities. I took some pictures of that pretty flower and brought out the rosary from the previous year. Slow tears came as I KNEW my beloved had something to do with this!!

The next year on my birthday I was ready. I kept my eyes open and watched the mailbox closely. Once again, I was gifted with a tiny prayer book from another unknown charity!

That was my last birthday gift from Mark.

Three gifts in three years. Three to represent our three children?

These extraordinary experiences are ones I'm still unwrapping and understanding.

I continue to learn and grow from my experiences. I am so grateful!! Nature is my guide and I receive nature's gifts daily.

Today I received one more gift from Mark as I got this manuscript ready for the editor.

I took this picture at 7:12 am. Do you know the significance of 7:12? It just so happens to be Mark's Birthday, July 12th.

I love you.

Margaret

About the Author

This is the first publication for Margaret Stoiber, RN. After becoming a widow unexpectedly at age 44, her focus in life shifted dramatically and CPR for The Grieving Heart is the result of half-written notebooks, scattered papers, many crumpled napkins and natural observations along her path of healing.

To learn more about how Margaret is helping the bereaved, please visit her website cprforthegrievingheart.com. You will find advice from other widows, a guided meditation for healing, helpful hints on compassionate ways to communicate at a funeral and much more.

Printed in the USA
CPSIA information can be obtained
at www.ICGtesting.com
JSHW011446141023
49894JS00011B/46